THE
GLOW-IN-THE-DARK
BOOK OF
HUMAN
SKELETONS

BY MICHAEL NOVAK
ILLUSTRATED BY KATE SWEENEY

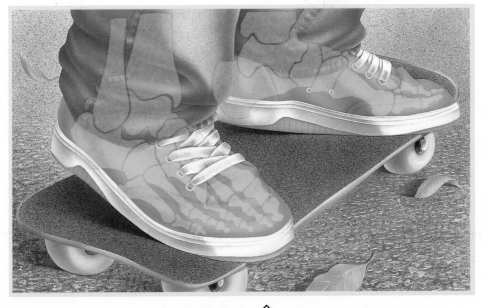

Random House 🏠 New York

http://www.randomhouse.com/
Library of Congress Cataloging-in-Publication Data
Novak, Michael. The glow-in-the-dark book of human skeletons / by Michael Novak ;
illustrated by Kate Sweeney. p. cm. ISBN 0-679-85646-3 I. Body, Human—Juvenile literature.
[1. Body, Human.] I. Sweeney, Kate, ill. II. Title. III. Series. QP37.N59 1997 612—dc20 94-47304
Printed in Taiwan 10 9 8 7 6 5 4 3 2 1

You can't see your skeleton—but you'd be in big trouble without it! You wouldn't be able to ride a skateboard or swing on the monkey bars. You'd just lie around like a puddle of goo!

Bones are lightweight but strong. They give your body its shape and protect your insides. Together with your muscles, they allow you to do things no other creature on earth can do.

Your skull acts like a crash helmet for your brain. It feels like one big bone when you touch it, but it's not. Your skull is actually made of 29 separate bones that fit together like a jigsaw puzzle. But only one of them can move. Can you guess which one it is?

When a baby is born, its skull bones aren't fully joined together. That's because the brain is still growing—it will triple in size in the first few years—and the skull bones have to leave it room to grow.

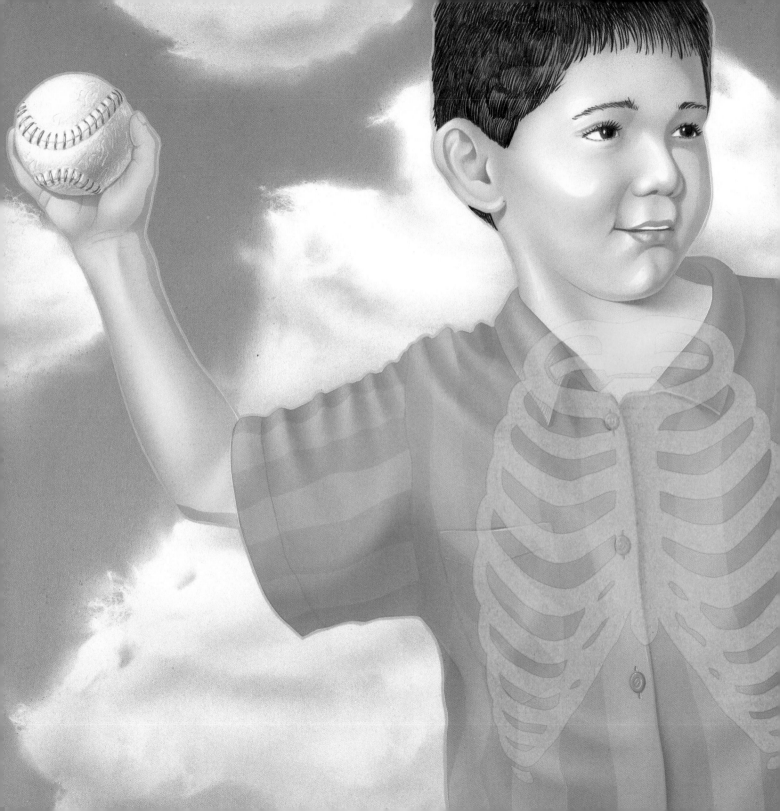

Most people have 12 pairs of ribs (some have 13). Ribs form a sturdy cage around your heart and lungs, but they move just enough to help keep you alive. Each time you breathe in, your ribs move up and out, lifting up your lungs. This motion helps your lungs expand so they can suck in the air you need.

And the ribs never seem to wear out. By the time you are 21, you will have taken more than 100 million breaths!

Your ribs are attached to your spine, or backbone—a column of 26 small bones that you can feel with your fingers. Each bone moves only a little, like the links in a chain, but this gives the whole spine great flexibility.

The place where two bones meet is called a joint. Your shoulder is a ball-and-socket joint. It works like a joystick, letting you swing your arm all the way through a full circle. But shoulders pay a price for being so agile—they are the joints most likely to dislocate, or pop out of joint.

The joint at your elbow is called a hinge joint. Like the hinges on a door, it allows your arm to move back and forth—but not around in a circle. Your elbow can twist sideways just a bit, though. Try it—your two lower arm bones will swivel, or rotate, over each other at the upper and lower ends.

A hinge joint (right) is stronger but more limited than a ball-and-socket joint (left).

Nearly half the bones in your body are in your hands and feet—there are 27 in each hand alone. (More about your feet later.) These bones are small but mighty. Together they form a system of levers and pincers that lets you make an incredible range of movements—from squeezing orange juice to picking up a pin to playing the piano.

Only gorillas, chimpanzees, and some monkeys have opposable thumbs like us.

Unlike most animals, humans have opposable thumbs—thumbs that can oppose, or touch, every other fingertip. It's the most important feature of the human hand. To see this for yourself, spend a day without using your thumb. Start by trying to peel a banana.

The strongest joints in your body are in your hips, at the place where the hips meet the upper leg bones, or thighbones. Like the joints in your shoulders, the hip joints let you swing your legs from front to back and, in a more limited way than your shoulders, from side to side. Your hip joints, along with the thick muscles that surround them, support your body weight as you walk around. You can even support yourself on one leg.

Humans are the only animals that can walk comfortably on two legs. That's because our pelvis, or hipbone, sits upright, which keeps our spine and legs in a straight line as we walk.

The human hipbone looks like a big bowl with a hole in the bottom. Unlike chimps or birds, we can stand upright for hours.

Other animals can totter on their back legs for a short time, but their hipbones tilt forward. Sooner or later, they have to drop back down on all fours.

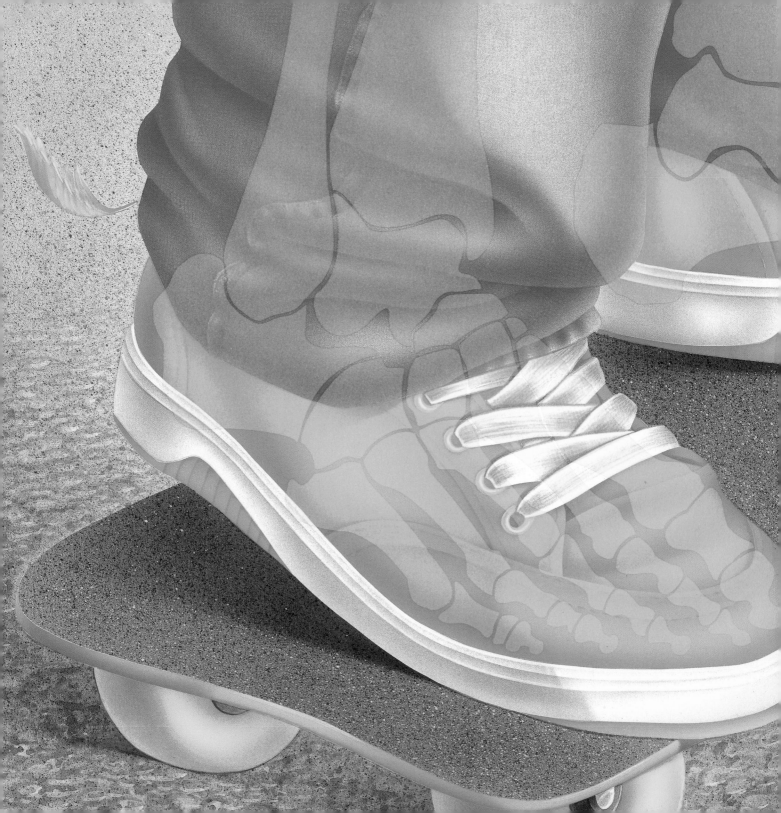

The 26 bones in your foot and ankle look a lot like the bones of your hands, but your feet don't move as freely as your hands do. And, unlike your thumb, your big toe is not opposable.

But your long, broad feet have an important job. They carry the weight of your entire body. The arch, or curve, on the bottom of each foot gives your body a springy base to push off from when you are walking. And each toe—even the tiny "pinkie" toe—grips the ground with each step and helps you keep your balance.

Your toe bones look a lot like your finger bones, except that many of them are hidden inside your foot.

Your skeleton will change a lot in your lifetime. When you were born, your body had about 350 bones. By the time you're fully grown, it will have only about 206. Do the other bones disappear? No. As you grow, many bones join together to form bigger bones.

The bones of your feet grow faster than any other bone in your body. Your feet reach their final size long before the rest of you does.

Girls grow faster than boys but finish their growing first, by the age of 12 or 14.

As you get older, your bones become more brittle and tend to break more easily.

Here are the main bones of the body and their scientific names—so you can "bone up" on your bones!

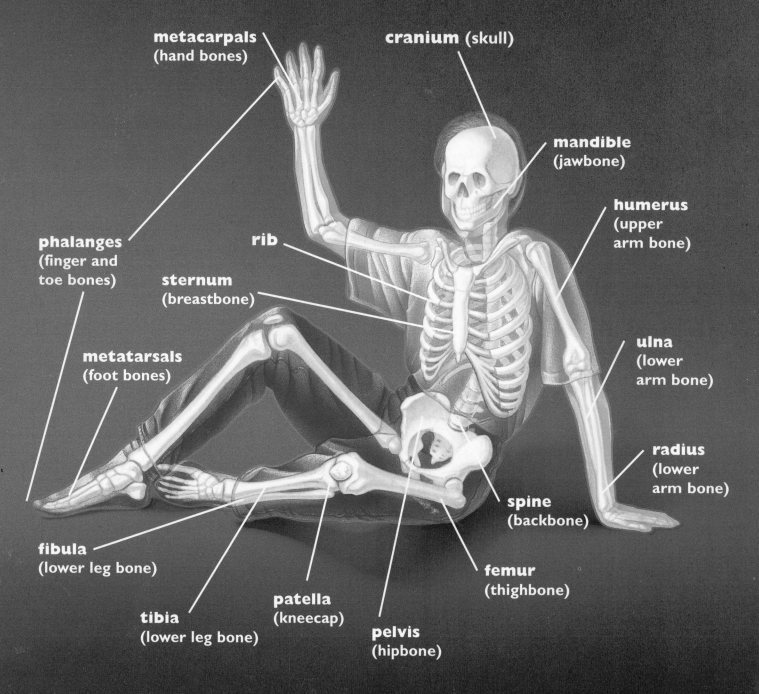

metacarpals (hand bones)

cranium (skull)

mandible (jawbone)

humerus (upper arm bone)

phalanges (finger and toe bones)

rib

sternum (breastbone)

ulna (lower arm bone)

metatarsals (foot bones)

radius (lower arm bone)

spine (backbone)

fibula (lower leg bone)

femur (thighbone)

tibia (lower leg bone)

patella (kneecap)

pelvis (hipbone)